Let Freedom Ring

Abraham Lincoln

by Lora Polack Oberle

Consultant:
Steven M. Wilson, Assistant Director and Curator
Abraham Lincoln Library and Museum
Harrogate, Tennessee

Bridgestone Books
an imprint of Capstone Press
Mankato, Minnesota

Bridgestone Books are published by Capstone Press,
151 Good Counsel Drive • P.O. Box 669 • Mankato, Minnesota 56002.
www.capstonepress.com

Printed in the United States of America.

Library of Congress Cataloging-in-Publication Data
Oberle, Lora Polack.
    Abraham Lincoln / by Lora Oberle.
        p. cm. — (Let freedom ring)
    Includes bibliographic references and index.
    ISBN 0-7368-1086-2 (hardcover)
    ISBN 0-7368-4522-4 (paperback)
    1. Lincoln, Abraham, 1809–1865—Juvenile literature. 2. Presidents—United States—
Biography—Juvenile literature. [1. Lincoln, Abraham, 1809–1865. 2. Presidents.]
I. Title. II. Series.
E457.905 .O24 2002
973.7'092—dc21   2001003060
                                                                       CIP

Summary: Examines the life of Abraham Lincoln, considered to be one of the United States'
    greatest presidents. Traces his roots as a poor farmer, his rise through politics, and his
    critical decisions during the U.S. Civil War. Also looks at him as a family man and
    explores his continuing effect on the modern world.

Editorial Credits
Charles Pederson, editor; Kia Bielke, cover designer, interior layout designer, and illustrator;
Deirdre Barton, photo researcher

Photo Credits
Cover: Hulton/Archive Photos; CORBIS, 5, 23, 24, 37, 43; Stock Montage, Inc., 7, 9;
North Wind Pictures, 8, 11, 16, 30, 32, 38 (large); Hulton/Archive Photos, 12; George
Eastman House/Alexander Hesler/Hulton/Archive Photos, 15; Archive Photos, 18, 38 (small);
National Portrait Gallery, Smithsonian Institution/Magnum, 19; Bettmann/CORBIS, 27;
Stock Montage/Hulton/Archive Photos, 29, 42; Scala/Art Resource, NY, 34–35; Digital
Stock, 41

1 2 3 4 5 6 07 06 05 04 03 02

Table of Contents

Chapter One

The Best President

As the 16th U.S. president, Abraham Lincoln led the United States through the tragedy of the U.S. Civil War (1861–1865). Abraham was determined to keep the United States together. He did not want the Southern states to secede from, or leave, the United States. Yet the states did secede, leading to war.

For four years, Americans fought Americans. About 620,000 American soldiers died during the bitter fighting. More Americans died in the Civil War than in all U.S. wars from the Revolutionary War (1775–1783) to the Vietnam War (1954–1975).

Abraham had to overcome many challenges. He grew up poor in the American West. He had less than a year of formal schooling and no combat experience to guide him as a military leader. But he found the strength to become what many people consider the best American president ever.

Abraham Lincoln led the United States during the Civil War. Many people consider him to be the best U.S. president.

Chapter Two

Rising above Difficulties

On Sunday, February 12, 1809, Abraham Lincoln was born in a one-room log cabin in Hardin County, Kentucky. His parents were Thomas and Nancy Hanks Lincoln. Not much is known about Nancy Lincoln. Abraham remembered her as thin and sad eyed and later called her his "angel mother."

Abraham's father was Thomas Lincoln. As a poorly educated farmhand, Thomas mostly worked with his hands.

In Abraham's seventh year, the Lincolns loaded their possessions and headed for Pigeon Creek, Indiana. Pigeon Creek lay about 100 miles (160 kilometers) north of Hardin County. Thomas built a one-room cabin with an open attic area, where Abraham slept. The new home was in a thick, wild forest. At night, Abraham heard wolves howl and mountain lions scream.

The illustration above shows the cabin where Abraham and his family lived when he was a child.

Sarah Bush Lincoln

Sarah Bush Lincoln (right) provided a secure home for Abraham. His years with her were some of the happiest of his life.

To clear the land for farming, Thomas taught Abraham to chop with an ax. Over time, Abraham became expert at chopping. Thomas even rented Abraham to chop for others for 25 cents a day.

In 1818, 34-year-old Nancy Lincoln died of a disease called milk sickness. Cows ate poisonous plants, and people who drank the cows' milk became sick. After seven days in bed with a fever, Nancy died. After Nancy's death, Abraham's sister Sarah, age 11, did her best to cook and clean for Abraham and Thomas.

The next year, Thomas returned to Kentucky to marry Sarah Bush Johnston. She came with him to Illinois to care for the Lincolns. Sarah brought furniture and bedding. The Lincolns had never had such luxuries. These years with warm, loving Sarah Bush Lincoln were happy ones for Abraham.

Learning

When Abraham could, he went to school—a week here, a month there. He loved to learn and read anything. He read the works of William Shakespeare, the Bible, and books about George Washington.

Abraham developed his gift for public speaking. He practiced speeches for his friends. His funny stories became famous.

Abraham (left) read books whenever he had the chance.

Honest Abe

Many people knew Abraham by the nickname "Honest Abe." There are many stories about Abraham's honesty. Some people say that once, he realized he had charged a customer six cents too much at a store he owned. Abraham walked about 6 miles (10 kilometers) to the customer's house to return the six cents.

As a lawyer, Abraham never charged a customer more than he thought the person could pay. Once, he made his law partner return half of a customer's fees. Abraham claimed that their services had not been worth that much money.

A New Life in New Salem

In 1831, Abraham moved to New Salem, Illinois. He worked in a general store. At night, he slept in the back of the store. He quickly made friends.

About that time, people feared that Black Hawk, an American Indian leader, wanted to begin a war. The town chose Abraham to lead its local militia. These volunteers were ready but never needed to fight. Abraham later joked that his three months of military service amounted only to "bloody battles with mosquitoes." Other U.S. soldiers defeated Black Hawk and his followers.

Politician and Lawyer

After eight months in New Salem, Abraham ran for his first public office. He lost the election. In 1834, at age 25, Abraham ran for the Illinois House of Representatives, the state lawmaking body. This time he won.

The legislature did not pay well, so Abraham needed another job. A friend suggested that Abraham become a lawyer. Abraham borrowed

The painting at left shows a battle during the Black Hawk War (1832). Abraham was ready to fight in the war, but he never saw combat.

some law books and studied whenever he could. People often saw him sitting under a tree reading or walking along a road repeating law passages.

All lawyers had to pass a test before they could practice law. In 1837, Abraham passed the test and became a lawyer in Springfield, Illinois. The 28-year-old Abraham finally had the chance to earn a living with his mind instead of with physical labor.

Love and Marriage

In 1839, Abraham met Mary Todd, the daughter of a wealthy slave-holding Kentucky family. Mary was well educated. She spoke French and enjoyed

Mary Todd (right) and Abraham married in 1842.

discussing politics with Abraham. The two spent many hours talking about poetry, too. They fell in love.

The couple had many life changes. They married on November 4, 1842. Their first child, Robert, was born a year later. Mary's father helped the young couple buy a house in Springfield. This was the only house Abraham ever owned. Here, three more children were born: Edward (1846), William (1850), and Thomas (1853), also called "Tad." Edward died in 1850 after a long illness.

Politics

In 1846, Illinois voters elected Abraham to the U.S. House of Representatives. He opposed the Mexican War (1846–1848) and did not win the next election.

Abraham returned to Springfield and became a successful lawyer. In the 1850s, his income reached $5,000 a year, three times the income of the governor of Illinois.

In 1855, Abraham ran for the U.S. Senate but lost. In 1858, he ran for a new political party, the Republicans. Republican leaders founded the party to fight slavery, an issue that deeply divided the country.

Chapter Three

A Country Divided

In the North, slavery was neither legal nor necessary for the Northern economy. Most white Northerners like Abraham disliked slavery. Yet they did not fully accept free African Americans. In some Northern states, for example, African Americans could not vote, hold political office, or sit on juries.

In the South, slavery was legal and central to Southern life. Large farms called plantations and some smaller farms depended on free slave labor to plant and harvest cotton, a major crop. Slaves did jobs around the house and took care of their owners.

An uneasy peace existed between the North and South. Most Northerners were willing to allow slavery if it remained only in the South. But new territories and states were opening out West. People wondered if those states would allow slavery. Any new state, slave or nonslave, could change the balance of government power in Washington, D.C.

Abraham (above, in 1860) hated slavery. Before the Civil War, however, he was not ready to abolish, or ban, it.

The slavery issue heated up in 1854 when the Kansas-Nebraska Act passed. U.S. law had banned slavery north of Missouri, but the act changed that ban. The act allowed each new state to decide for itself whether to be a slave state or nonslave state. Proslavery and antislavery settlers moved into Kansas to give their side more voters. The territory became known as "Bleeding Kansas" because of violence over slavery. The Kansas-Nebraska Act upset Northerners who did not want slavery to spread.

Abraham (with arm raised) debated Stephen Douglas (in blue, behind Abraham) seven times. The men focused on slavery issues.

Views on Slaves and Slavery

Abraham believed that slavery was wrong, but he did not think the U.S. government could ban, or abolish, slavery. He wanted slavery to have a "natural death." He did not want it to spread from the South into new states. Many people believed cotton farming would slowly exhaust the land. As cotton farming ended, the need for slaves would decrease, and slavery would end.

Many Northerners believed that African Americans were not equal to whites. Abraham may have agreed with this belief. He urged Illinois lawmakers to keep African Americans out of the state.

Yet, Abraham was a skilled politician. By voting to exclude African Americans from Illinois, he may have hoped to avoid upsetting the people who voted for him.

The Lincoln-Douglas Debates

Stephen Douglas, a U.S. senator from Illinois, was the author of the Kansas-Nebraska Act. In 1858, he ran for reelection. Abraham decided to oppose him.

During the campaign, Abraham and Douglas debated the slavery issue seven times. Douglas argued that a state's settlers should decide the issue themselves. Abraham said that all Americans, not individual states, should decide. Neither man wanted to abolish slavery immediately. Both men clearly stated that whites were superior to African Americans. Most of their audience agreed.

Abraham won national attention for his debate arguments, but he lost the election. After the election, Abraham traveled across the country to speak against slavery.

Elected President

Many men ran for president in the election of 1860. The antislavery Republican Party chose Abraham to be its candidate. Three men from other political parties also ran for president.

On election night, November 6, 1860, Abraham learned that he had been elected president. He received only 40 percent of the votes. At the time, this result made him the least popular president ever elected. But the other candidates took votes from each other, leaving Abraham the winner. He told his wife, "Mary, we are elected."

Family in the White House

The Lincoln sons were the first president's children to live in the White House. Abraham and Mary raised their boys with much love and little punishment. They liked the boys to have fun. Abraham enjoyed spending time with his sons. He wrestled with them in his office. He allowed them to interrupt meetings. He even brought them with him to visit the troops.

Robert (below left) was the oldest. In 1861, at age 17, he left to study at Harvard University. For Willie (next to Abraham), age 10, and Tad (at Mary's feet, right), age 7, the White House was a playground. They played on the White House roof. They kept dogs, cats, rabbits, and other animals. In the halls, the boys raced their pet goats. One goat even slept in Tad's bedroom.

On February 20, 1862, Willie died after a two-week illness. Abraham had sometimes been depressed before. Willie's death left Abraham with the deepest depression of his life.

Chapter Four

Civil War

Abraham's election victory caused panic in the South. Southern leaders believed that Abraham would abolish slavery and destroy their way of life. They did not want to accept Abraham as president and began to move toward secession from the North, or Union.

On February 4, 1861, seven states formed a new country, the Confederate States of America. Many people expected the remaining Southern states to secede. Some people blamed Abraham for the breakup of the United States.

On March 4, 1861, Abraham officially became president. In his inaugural, or first, speech, Abraham said that he did not plan to end slavery in the South. But he reminded Southerners that he had promised to "preserve, protect, and defend" the United States. To him, the promise meant not letting states secede.

Two weeks after taking office, Abraham's first crisis arose. The South Carolina governor demanded that Abraham give the Confederacy Fort Sumter, a U.S. Army base in Charleston, South Carolina.

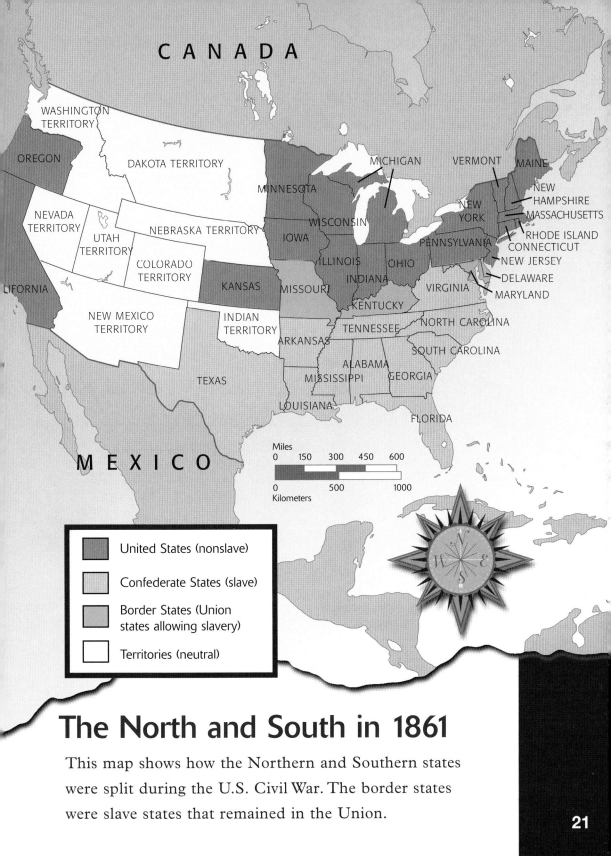

CANADA

WASHINGTON
TERRITORY

OREGON

DAKOTA TERRITORY

MINNESOTA

MICHIGAN

VERMONT

MAINE

NEW
HAMPSHIRE

NEVADA
TERRITORY

UTAH
TERRITORY

NEBRASKA TERRITORY

IOWA

WISCONSIN

NEW
YORK

MASSACHUSETTS

RHODE ISLAND

CONNECTICUT

COLORADO
TERRITORY

ILLINOIS

OHIO

PENNSYLVANIA

NEW JERSEY

CALIFORNIA

KANSAS

MISSOURI

INDIANA

KENTUCKY

VIRGINIA

DELAWARE

MARYLAND

NEW MEXICO
TERRITORY

INDIAN
TERRITORY

ARKANSAS

TENNESSEE

NORTH CAROLINA

SOUTH CAROLINA

TEXAS

MISSISSIPPI

ALABAMA

GEORGIA

LOUISIANA

FLORIDA

MEXICO

Miles
0   150   300   450   600

0   500   1000
Kilometers

United States (nonslave)

Confederate States (slave)

Border States (Union
states allowing slavery)

Territories (neutral)

The North and South in 1861

This map shows how the Northern and Southern states
were split during the U.S. Civil War. The border states
were slave states that remained in the Union.

Abraham refused. The Confederates cut off food to the fort. They hoped the soldiers would leave the fort when they ran out of food.

Abraham still hoped to avoid a war. But instead of removing U.S. troops, he sent them food. On April 12, 1861, Confederate troops began shooting at Fort Sumter and bombed it for almost 36 hours. The Civil War had begun.

The Union seemed to have advantages over the Confederacy. It had 23 states and 22 million people. The 11 Southern states had only 9 million people. Of these, 4 million were slaves and could not be in the army. The North had a navy, and the Confederacy did not. The North had more industry to produce weapons and ammunition.

But the Confederate states had important advantages. First, some of the country's best military leaders had joined the Southern army. Second, they would fight on familiar ground.

The First Battle

On July 21, 1861, Union and Confederate troops fought for the first time at Manassas, Virginia. This important railroad center lay near Bull Run Creek,

A Tall Man

Abraham (center) stood 6 feet, 4 inches (1.93 meters) tall. The stovepipe hat he often wore added another 8 inches (20 centimeters) to his height. In his hat, Abraham towered above the crowd at 7 feet (2.13 meters).

about 25 miles (40 kilometers) southwest of Washington, D.C.

Union generals expected to win this first battle at Bull Run. Their goal was to sweep on to the Confederate capital of Richmond, Virginia, and finish the war quickly. People rode out from Washington, D.C., to watch the expected Northern victory. Some even brought a picnic lunch.

Abraham waited in Washington, D.C., for news of the battle. Soon, he learned that the

Confederates had defeated his Union armies. The first major battle of the war was a Union disaster.

A Plan to Win the War

The Union created a three-part plan to win the war. In the South, the navy would blockade Confederate ports so they could get no supplies from other countries. In the West, the army wanted to control the Mississippi River. In the East, the army planned to capture Richmond and other Confederate cities.

Abraham turned to General George McClellan to lead the armies. Abraham wanted to

In 1861, Union General George McClellan (right) was Abraham's best hope to win the Civil War.

attack swiftly, but McClellan was cautious. For months, he trained his troops but did not fight.

By the spring of 1862, the war plan was unfolding. The navy effectively blockaded Southern ports. The Union Army was gaining control of the Mississippi River. In the East, however, McClellan's troops failed to capture Richmond. At the same time, Confederate troops defeated Union soldiers in Virginia's Shenandoah River valley. The Union had yet to win a battle in the East.

Freeing the Slaves

Abraham had a new strategy to announce. He planned to free slaves in areas that Confederate forces held. This Emancipation Proclamation waited only for a Union victory.

In the summer and fall of 1862, battle news was bad for the North. Among other fights, a second Battle of Bull Run was a major Union defeat.

In mid-September, Confederate troops under General Robert E. Lee invaded the border state of Maryland. Union troops fought Lee's army at Antietam Creek near Sharpsburg, Maryland.

The Emancipation Proclamation

When the Civil War began, Abraham did not necessarily intend to free any slaves. He wanted only to keep the South from seceding. As the war went on, however, he saw that freeing the slaves was necessary. Many slaves were eager to fight, and the Union armies could use fresh soldiers. Abraham issued the Emancipation Proclamation, an order that the Union armies were to help free slaves by any means.

How to free the slaves was a delicate issue. Some slave states had remained in the Union. These border states of Kentucky, Missouri, Maryland, and Delaware were important in the war against the South. Abraham did not want to anger these states. The Emancipation Proclamation solved the problem by freeing slaves only in areas under Confederate control. The proclamation went into effect on January 1, 1863.

Thousands of soldiers died on this single bloodiest day of the war. Lee retreated to Virginia. McClellan, always cautious, did not follow.

Though not complete, the Battle of Antietam was enough of a victory for Abraham. On September 22, 1862, he announced that starting January 1, 1863, the Union Army would free slaves in Confederate-held areas. In the rest of the Union, slavery remained as it was. Maryland and Missouri, for example, could keep their slaves.

People all over North America reacted to the proclamation. Confederates hated it. Most Northerners supported it. Abolitionists and African Americans were glad. Thousands of slaves tried to escape as soon as they heard about it.

The painting above shows Abraham (third from left) reading the Emancipation Proclamation to the members of his government.

Chapter Five

The Country's Darkest Days

In June 1863, General Lee again pushed north, into Pennsylvania. Abraham chose a different army general, George Meade, to oppose Lee. After fierce fighting at the Battle of Gettysburg from July 1 to 3, Meade finally defeated Lee. However, as McClellan had done, Meade allowed Lee to retreat.

The battle was the war's turning point. Lee's army was too weak afterward to threaten the North.

Gettysburg was the bloodiest battle of the Civil War. More than 51,000 soldiers died in those three days. So many people died that there was no time to move the bodies to a cemetery. They had to be quickly buried where they had fallen.

The Gettysburg Address

Gettysburg's town leaders decided to create a new national cemetery on the battlefield. They invited Abraham to speak at the dedication on November 19, 1863. That day,

The Battle of Gettysburg (above) was the turning point of the Civil War.

Myth vs. Fact

Myth: Abraham wrote the Gettysburg Address on the back of an envelope.

Fact: Abraham was a careful writer. He began working on his speech in Washington, D.C., several days before delivering it. Five copies of the Gettysburg Address still exist. Below, Abraham is shown delivering the speech.

Abraham gave his most famous speech, the Gettysburg Address. The two-minute speech began, "Four score and seven years ago, our fathers brought forth, upon this continent, a new nation, conceived in liberty and dedicated to the proposition [idea] that all men are created equal."

The speech put the suffering of the Civil War in a larger view. Abraham said the North fought the war to preserve America's experiment in democracy.

Though the Union won at Gettysburg, the war was wearing Abraham down. He said that being president was killing him. He looked older, had trouble sleeping, and fought depression.

Abraham Finds His General

On July 4, 1863, the Union Army, under General Ulysses S. Grant, won an important victory in the West. Union troops captured Vicksburg, Mississippi, the last strongly defended Confederate city on the Mississippi River. Afterward, the Union controlled the entire river.

Grant, the hero of Vicksburg, was to be the general who could win the war. On March 9, 1864, Abraham appointed him to lead all Union forces.

Together, Abraham and Grant planned to finish the war. In the East, Grant pushed toward Richmond. In the South, General William Tecumseh Sherman advanced from Tennessee to Georgia. Grant had ordered him to destroy Atlanta, Georgia.

A Second Term

The presidential election of 1864 was historic. The voters had not reelected an American president in the past 30 years. Abraham wanted to stay in office. He felt that it was his duty to see the war to its end.

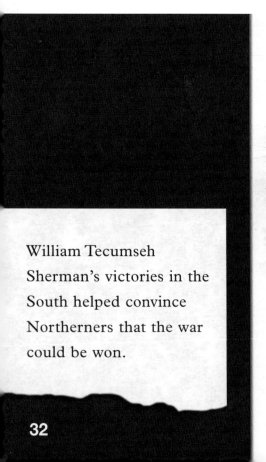

William Tecumseh Sherman's victories in the South helped convince Northerners that the war could be won.

The election of 1864 was difficult. News writers called Abraham a "beast" and "murderer" for his role in the war. Many voters were unhappy with Abraham. They were tired of the fighting and the death. Some blamed Abraham for causing the war. Some were angry about the Emancipation Proclamation. His biggest supporters were African Americans, but they could not vote. Many people believed Abraham would lose the election.

But in the late summer and fall of 1864, Union forces scored a series of victories. Sherman's troops captured Atlanta after long and bloody fighting. Other victories came in the Shenandoah River valley in Virginia and at the city of Mobile, Alabama. Finally, Northerners could see the end of the war, and they gave Abraham the credit.

Abraham won the election. Soldiers cheered when they heard the news. Abraham took the victory as public approval to finish the war.

The Emancipation Proclamation was a wartime measure. Abraham knew that Congress could easily undo it after the war. The only way to outlaw slavery permanently was by amending, or changing, the U.S. Constitution. Abraham worked hard to persuade Congress to make such a change. On January 31, 1865, Congress passed the 13th Amendment. It banned slavery in the entire United States forever.

Wrapping Up the War

On March 4, 1865, Abraham officially became president for the second time. He spoke of his vision of postwar healing. He urged his fellow Northerners not to hate the Southerners who had fought them. "With malice [hatred] toward none,..." he said, "let us...bind up the nation's wounds."

At the same time, Union forces were sweeping toward final victory. Sherman captured Savannah, Georgia, and then Charleston, where the war had begun almost four years earlier. On April 3, 1865, Union troops finally entered Richmond.

The next day, Abraham and his son Tad toured Richmond. Parts of the defeated city had burned during the fighting. Some buildings were still smoking. Former slaves, celebrating their freedom, ran to greet Abraham.

Abraham and Tad walked to the home of Jefferson Davis. The Confederate president had left a day earlier. Union soldiers cheered as Abraham entered the building and sat at Davis's desk.

On April 9, General Lee surrendered his troops at Appomattox, Virginia. The rest of the Confederates followed. The war was over.

Union troops approached Richmond on April 2, 1865. While the city burned, many residents chose to escape across the James River.

Chapter Six

He Belongs to the Ages

As the war ended, Abraham's advisors worried about his safety. They were afraid that Confederate supporters might kidnap or assassinate him. Almost every day, Abraham received letters that threatened his death. He kept the letters in a file that was marked "Assassinations."

On April 14, 1865, Abraham and Mary Lincoln went to Ford's Theatre in Washington, D.C. They were going to see a play, *Our American Cousin*. The Lincolns and another couple sat in a private box in a balcony to one side of the stage.

Only one guard accompanied the president. The guard sat outside the box by the door. During the play, the guard went for a drink at a bar next door, leaving the president unprotected.

During act three of the play, the door to the box burst open. A shadowy figure entered, aimed a small gun at the back of Abraham's head,

The photo above shows the theater box where Abraham was shot
shortly after the Civil War ended. The chair in which Abraham
sat is visible in the box to the right.

and fired. The assassin jumped from the box onto the stage and ran from the theater. Abraham slumped forward in his chair as Mary screamed. He lived until the next day but never awoke or spoke again.

The killer was John Wilkes Booth, a popular actor who supported the South. By killing the president, Booth hoped to give the South a chance to continue the war. Union troops cornered Booth in a Virginia barn 12 days later. They shot and killed him as they tried to capture him.

Thousands of people came to Abraham's funeral (right). His death moved people to write music in his memory (above).

"Who Is Dead?"

In early April 1865, near the end of the Civil War, Abraham had a strange dream. He told his wife and some friends that in the dream, he heard someone crying. He wandered through the White House looking for the source of the sound.

Finally, he saw a coffin surrounded by people dressed in black. "Who is dead?" Abraham asked.

"The president," a soldier replied. "Killed by an assassin." Abraham's dream came true just days later.

Death and Funeral

The news of Abraham's death on April 15, 1865, shocked the country. Businesses shut down. Adults cried. Only the day before, the North had been celebrating the end of the war. Now, people did not know what would happen as Abraham's vice president, Andrew Johnson, became president.

Some Southerners were glad at the news, but most were not. They felt ashamed and sorry that Booth had killed Abraham in their name. Even Jefferson Davis was shocked.

Abraham's funeral took place in the White House on April 19, 1865. Mary was too upset to attend, but Robert Lincoln stood silently by his father's coffin. A funeral procession brought the coffin to the U.S. Capitol, where thousands of people silently passed it. Many waited hours to say farewell.

Abraham's Last Journey

Friends in Springfield, Illinois, requested that Abraham be buried there. His coffin was placed on a special funeral train that also carried a coffin with his son Willie's body. The train followed much the same route that Abraham had traveled from Springfield to Washington, D.C., four years earlier.

The train stopped in some towns, allowing long lines of waiting people to pass the president's coffin. In rural areas, people waited by the tracks for the train to pass. Some placed flowers on the tracks. People even waited for the train at night, building large fires to keep warm.

Abraham had led the nation through its worst conflict. He had freed the slaves. Now, he was gone as the country faced two difficult tasks. One was healing the wounds of war and bringing North and

South together again. The other was bringing the freed slaves into the larger society. Other leaders would have to guide the nation through these tasks.

Many people consider Abraham to be the United States' best president. His speeches express the country's greatest ideals of freedom and justice. His words and example continue to inspire leaders and other people everywhere.

The Lincoln Memorial in Washington, D.C., captures Abraham's strength and caring for North and South.

TIMELINE

Abraham's Life

Born in Kentucky

Nancy Hanks Lincoln dies.

Moves to New Salem, Illinois

Elected to his first public office in the Illinois House of Representatives

Marries Mary Todd

Elected to the U.S. House of Representatives

1809   1818   1831   1834   1842   1846   1854

Historical Events

Kansas-Nebraska Act passes, allowing territories to vote on slavery.

Elected president for the second time

April 14: Shot by John Wilkes Booth; April 15: dies.

Elected president for the first time

| 1858 | 1860 | 1861 | 1862 | 1863 | 1864 | 1865 |

Lincoln-Douglas debates

April: Confederate troops fire on Fort Sumter to begin Civil War; July: First Battle of Bull Run.

Emancipation Proclamation announced

Congress approves 13th Amendment to end slavery; Richmond falls to Union forces; Lee surrenders.

Grant accepts command of Union armies.

July: Battle of Gettysburg; November: Gettysburg Address.

Glossary

abolish (uh-BOL-ish)—to make illegal or get rid of

amend (uh-MEND)—to change

assassination (uh-sass-uh-NAY-shuhn)—the murder of someone who is well-known or important, such as a president

border state (BOR-dur STATE)—one of the slave states that remained in the Union during the Civil War

Confederacy (kuhn-FED-ur-uh-see)—the Southern slave-holding states that left the Union during the Civil War

Emancipation Proclamation (i-man-suh-PAY-shuhn prok-luh-MAY-shuhn)—an order to free slaves in Confederate areas

inaugural speech (in-AWG-yuh-ruhl SPEECH)—first formal speech of a public official beginning a new term of office

Kansas-Nebraska Act (KAN-zuhss nuh-BRASS-kuh AKT)—a law that allowed each new state to decide for itself whether to allow slavery

plantation (plan-TAY-shuhn)—a large farm that usually grows one main crop such as cotton or tobacco

secede (suh-SEED)—to formally withdraw from a group or organization, often to form another organization

13th Amendment (THUR-teenth uh-MEND-muhnt)—an amendment to the U.S. Constitution that bans slavery in the United States

Union (YOON-yuhn)—the states that remained loyal to the federal government during the Civil War

For Further Reading

Arnold, James R. *On to Richmond: The Civil War in the East, 1861–1865.* Minneapolis: Lerner Publications Co., 2002.

Bowler, Sarah. *Abraham Lincoln: Our Sixteenth President.* Our Presidents. Chanhassen, Minn.: Child's World, 2002.

Carey, Charles W., Jr. *The Emancipation Proclamation.* Journey to Freedom. Chanhassen, Minn.: Child's World, 2000.

January, Brendan. *The Assassination of Abraham Lincoln.* Cornerstones of Freedom. New York: Children's Press, 1998.

Lincoln, Abraham. *Abraham Lincoln, the Writer: A Treasury of His Greatest Speeches and Letters.* Harold Holzer, ed. Honesdale, Pa.: Boyds Mills Press, 2000.

Marrin, Albert. *Commander in Chief Abraham Lincoln and the Civil War.* New York: Dutton Children's Books, 1997.

Sullivan, George. *Abraham Lincoln.* In Their Own Words. New York: Scholastic Reference, 2000.

Places of Interest

Abraham Lincoln Birthplace National Historic Site

Located near Hodgenville, Kentucky

http://www.nps.gov/abli/linchomj.htm

Abraham's birthplace

The Abraham Lincoln Library and Museum

120 Cumberland Gap Parkway

Harrogate, TN 37752

http://www.lmunet.edu/Museum/Index.html

Large collection of Abraham's belongings

Ford's Theatre National Historic Site

Near 10th and E Streets

Washington, D.C.

http://www.nps.gov/foth/index.htm

Site of Abraham's assassination

Lincoln Boyhood National Memorial

Lincoln City, IN 47552

http://www.nps.gov/libo/index.htm

Farm where Abraham grew up

Lincoln Home National Historic Site

426 South Seventh Street

Springfield, IL 62701-1901

http://www.nps.gov/liho/table.htm

The only home Abraham owned

Lincoln Memorial

On the National Mall

Washington, D.C.

http://www.nps.gov/linc/home.htm

Monument to the 16th president

Lincoln's New Salem State Historic Site

One-half hour northwest of Springfield

Petersburg, IL 62675

http://www.lincolnsnewsalem.com/home.cfm

Reconstructed village of Abraham's early adult years

Lincoln Tomb State Historic Site

Oak Ridge Cemetery

Springfield, IL 62702

http://www.state.il.us/hpa/Sites/LincolnTomb.htm

Burial place of the Lincoln family

Internet Sites

Do you want to learn more about Abraham Lincoln?
Visit the FactHound at *www.facthound.com*

FactHound can track down many sites to help you. All the
FactHound sites are hand-selected by our editors. FactHound will
fetch the best, most accurate information to answer your questions.

IT'S EASY! IT'S FUN!
1) Go to *www.facthound.com*
2) Type in: **0736810862**
3) Click on **FETCH IT** and FactHound will put you on the trail
   of several helpful links.

You can also search by subject or book title. So, relax
and let our pal FactHound do the research for you!

Index